20 GOLDEN LEADERSHIP NUGGETS

Practical leadership lessons to use today

by

Nicole F. Smith

20 Golden Leadership Nuggets: Practical leadership lessons to use today
by Nicole F. Smith

ISBN:

| 978-1-950336-09-8 | Print |
| 978-1-950336-07-4 | Ebook |

Dedication...and "Thank you!"

I dedicate this gem to my husband, Marcus, who supported me and knew of my passion and dream to share my golden leadership nuggets with others. You have shown me how to be an authentic and genuine leader even when I doubted my own self and capabilities.

To my two sons, Jordan and Justin – read up and learn your lessons! You are the next generation to lead the charge and I proudly know that you will do it with such boldness, courage, empathy, and strength.

Thank you to my mommy (Alice) and daddy (Tony) for being my cheerleaders and my listening ears as there were times I thought I was losing my marbles wondering if what I was seeing in the workplace was...well...real. More often than not, questioning the leadership (or lack of) that I was experiencing and wondering how to handle it...you listened and provided sound advice. And look – we made it through!

Of course, I thank every single leader or manager that has supplied me with all of my golden leadership nuggets! You have helped me grow in leaps and bounds and I appreciate **every single one of you.**

Table of Contents

Preface

It can be scary. It can be overwhelming. It can be immensely rewarding. What is this thing that can have people brimming with sometimes conflicting emotions? What is it that everyone believes will instantly give them the status and power they desire yet inspires so little interest in learning the good, bad, and ugly lessons?

Leadership.

This leadership journey that I have been on for the past 20 years has been one of many smiles, much laughter, a bucket of tears, and pockets full of golden nuggets. Some of these golden nuggets, 20 in particular, I have polished up to share with you.

Of course, you can learn about leadership from academic theories or from leadership consultants. However, the lessons that will drive all those theories home are the ones learned as you are applying them or observing others in the real world as a professional in a company, a volunteer in a charitable organization, or even a citizen in your community. Some of my best moves (as they say in sports) came from excellent real-life leaders that I had the honor of working for or working beside.

Additionally, behaviors that I witnessed and later realized were not "leadership traits" helped me create some of my best moves. These poor behaviors, condoned in the workplace, helped me develop my self-awareness and ability to adjust to meet others where they are. For that reason, I'm grateful even for the poor real-life leaders, because as you likely know, you can only change yourself as your self-awareness grows. Getting to know yourself will help you in relationships – in and out of the workplace.

As you grow during your leadership journey (mine started at a young 20 years old), you will backslide and second-guess yourself. There will be moments where you wonder if you are able to create followership and, once created, to maintain it. One shiny golden nugget I have learned is that leadership does take heart. It takes bravery, and it takes courage. As Mel Robbins states, "The more often that you choose courage, the more likely you'll succeed." Sounds easy, right? At the same time, it is so scary!

As Brené Brown writes in *Dare to Lead*, "Choose courage over comfort. Choose whole hearts over armor. And choose the great adventure of being brave and afraid. At the exact same time."

Many leaders are placed into leadership positions because they have proven themselves to be good at specific tasks. These tasks do not, unfortunately, include leading people. It is very flattering when you are promoted (or hired) to a leadership position. You have worked hard, and it indeed may be well-deserved. More often than not, the excitement of the promotion or the new role obscures the fact that you will now be leading people. More often than not, there is no leadership test, preparation, or mentor assigned to help guide this transition.

The million-dollar question looms: *Are you ready for something bigger than yourself, to see more talent and ability within your team than you have within yourself, and to accept the challenge of bringing it out?*

It is important to ask this question as you continue on your journey. I asked myself this question in every new leadership position I took on. I desired leadership for many reasons, but mostly, I wanted to be the leader that was in tune with the employees, the team, and their desires and talents. I want to lead authentically. Even today, I want to talk to them, empower them, push them, and dare to lead them!

Over 20 years ago, Lance Secretan wrote:

> *Leadership is not a formula or a program, it is a human activity that comes from the heart and considers the hearts of others.... If there is one thing a leader can do to connect with followers at a human, or better still a spiritual level, it is to become engaged with them fully, to share experiences and emotions, and to set aside the processes of leadership we have learned by rote.*

Twenty lessons over twenty years? These lessons are less than a fraction of the countless lessons I have learned. These 20 resonated for where I am as a leader today. I will certainly collect more golden nuggets in the days and weeks and years to come or dust off and polish up others that have been neglected in my pockets.

Remember, though, that these are golden nuggets that I have stumbled and fumbled upon in my journey. I have taken the good, the bad, and the ugly of those whom I reported to or observed in leadership throughout my career. I had many questions (and still do at times), took many notes, and made myself into a leader that helps bring to the table not only *my* best but also the best in others.

Wherever you are in your leadership journey, look out for golden nuggets. I offer these 20 to you to begin or to build your collection.

Know Yourself ... warts and all

If there was a proverb for leaders similar to the well-known proverb about doctors, that proverb would have to be "Leader, *know* thyself."

The popular proverb – *Physician, heal thyself* – taken at face value, suggests that doctors should not neglect self-care. Yet, medical schools and medical training programs principally teach doctors how to diagnose and treat their patients' symptoms with much less attention given to doctors acknowledging their own health problems. How confident would you feel taking advice from a doctor who is sniffling and sneezing during your whole appointment?

Similarly, the proverb I offer here – *Leader, know thyself* - taken at face value, suggests that leaders should not neglect self-knowledge. Yet, business schools and leadership training programs principally teach leaders how to determine and leverage their followers' motivations with much less attention given to leaders understanding their own psyche. How confident would you be taking direction from a leader who cannot fully explain why he or she has made a particular decision?

We can also compare the proverbs on a deeper level. Metaphorically, the well-known proverb means that before trying to advise or mend others, a person should *fix* his or her own imperfections. Likewise, my proverb suggests that before trying to influence or direct others, a person should *understand* his or her own imperfections.

For a leader to be effective, a journey of complete self-awareness is essential. I'll explain what I mean by "complete self-awareness" by first explaining what it is not. It is not just about knowing your strengths. It goes beyond simply identifying your strengths. Of course, having knowledge of your innate talents and enhancing them can improve your ability to lead, but being ignorant of your weaknesses can frustrate your development as a leader. Complete self-awareness also goes beyond recognizing and playing to your most comfortable leadership style. Of course, knowing your "go-to" approach is important (as I'll discuss in Lesson 20), but failing to understand why other approaches are less comfortable for you can reduce your adaptability as a leader. In the emotional intelligence field, self-awareness is most often described as an ability to recognize your own emotions and how they affect you. In my experience, complete self-awareness as a leader requires so much more.

What exactly, then, is complete self-awareness? I alluded earlier to leaders needing to have an awareness of their psyche and of their imperfections. Psyche, in its most generic sense, means a person's deepest thoughts, feelings, and beliefs. To this list, I would add your personality traits and general disposition, your preferred communication and conflict styles, your patterns of behavior, and your triggers and reactions. In a nutshell, you need a deep understanding of what makes you tick, especially when interacting with other people. Several self-assessment tools and professional assessments can help you begin this journey into the inner workings of your mind.

On the deep dive to develop complete self-awareness, you will discover dark aspects of your psyche; I promise you that if you have the courage to go deep enough, you will make unpleasant discoveries. These dark aspects are your imperfections, the flaws that, if not understood and tamed, can challenge your ability to be an effective leader. For example, you may discover that you are not naturally all that agreeable or that you prefer to avoid confrontation at all costs or that you micromanage after "delegating" or that you consistently get angry and lash out when someone insults your intelligence. You may discover biases or rigid beliefs about how things "should" be or irrational fears or self-limiting thoughts. It can be tempting to ignore these uncomfortable truths; discovering that we have imperfections is rarely pleasant.

Complete self-awareness means learning to know yourself, warts and all. Once you recognize your imperfections, you can develop newfound insight into challenging situations you repeatedly encounter as a leader. You can then decide how to work with these imperfections to overcome these challenges and become a more effective leader. For example, discovering how your deepest thoughts drive your feelings and beginning to recognize the physical cues that strong emotions are arising might help you to avoid or remove yourself from potentially explosive situations until you develop the self-control to defuse the thought pattern that triggers these emotions.

Complete self-awareness is essential for effective leadership, but, sadly, not every leader has this crucial capacity. Some have never even begun the deep dive, and others have stopped along the way fearing the darkness. Good leaders constantly push ahead, with courage, curiosity, and determination, on the journey to complete self-awareness, pausing from time to time to absorb new self-knowledge and to adjust their behavior accordingly.

The journey is long, even lifelong; it will not be easy, but if you want to be an effective leader, it is worth it.

There's More than One Way to Crack an Egg

Imagine the scene: You're in the kitchen at a friend's house chatting as he prepares to cook an omelet. He reaches for an egg and, with a firm grip on each end, he strikes the egg against the side of his mixing bowl. Or, maybe, he only holds the egg with one hand during this maneuver. Or, maybe, he strikes the egg against the edge of the counter. Perhaps, he holds the egg in one hand, picks up a knife with the other hand, and hits the egg firmly with the flat side of the knife.

You may look on in horror, shaking your head and thinking, "This guy has no idea what he's doing; the only right way to crack an egg is…." The truth is that any of these egg-cracking techniques will lead to success. Some may require more skill or practice, but the egg shells *will* be cracked, and the omelet *will* get made.

One of the biggest mistakes that people make is assuming that most other people act and think in the same way that they do. This assumption is an example of a flawed pattern of thinking known as a cognitive bias. The assumption is flawed because, as much as you might like for it to be true, everyone is not like you.

Leaders are not immune to the "everyone is like me" assumption. In fact, leaders often adopt a "my way or the highway" stance that transforms the cognitive bias into an unspoken workplace rule. Leaders who fall prey to what I'll call the "'my way' bias" often clash with or punish team members who don't do things the way they think they should be done or who have different ideas. By suppressing different thoughts and perspectives, these leaders lose a crucial element of diversity.

Some business situations *may* require unquestioning obedience – a PR crisis, legal or regulatory compliance, or financial reporting, to name a few. An off-script message, a questionable decision, or funny math could land the company in serious trouble. In these types of situations, enforcing "one right way" can be an appropriate and valuable leadership approach.

In most cases, however, enforcing a single way of thinking and acting will discourage team innovation and engagement. When you hire intelligent people, the hope is that they will feel empowered to contribute their unique talent and ideas to the success of the organization. Suggestions and behaviors that advance the team toward its overall objective should be encouraged even if they are a little different from what the leader might do.

Leaders who adopt an inclusive style of leadership can avoid the "my way" bias, tap into team creativity, and make all team members feel valued. Inclusive leadership means ideas and contributions from all team members are welcomed, heard, and considered; everyone's contributions are included when appropriate rather than being dismissed automatically simply because they are different from what the leader thinks or does.

The inclusive approach to leadership is a stark contrast to the "my way or the highway" approach. The older, more authoritarian style requires self-confidence – "I am right" – and constant supervision – "Are they doing what I told them to do how I told them to do it?" Not surprisingly, inclusive leadership requires different qualities and skills.

First, inclusive leadership requires complete self-awareness, as you learned in Lesson 1. Leaders must be aware of their general vulnerability to the "my way" bias and of their specific moments of weakness. Do you find it difficult to let team members find their own solutions when they are "too young"? Is it extremely important to you that non-urgent tasks be done in the exact order you would do them?

Being cognizant of your specific "my way" biases will help you begin to question their reasonableness. Is the whiz kid really too unintelligent or inexperienced to figure things out on her own? Does the internal memo on next month's department meeting agenda really need to be prepared before the slides for next month's pitch or vice versa? It is likely that the whiz kid will work out a solution that gets the job done and that both projects will be done on time. What is really bothering you may, in fact, be that these solutions or methods will not be perfect in your eyes.

This last realization is also crucial for inclusive leadership. Not everything will be perfect, as perfection is the enemy of good enough. If you're honest with yourself, you'll acknowledge that even your own ideas and methods are not perfect, at least not all the time. Likewise, other ideas and methods will not be perfect, but they will be good enough. "Good enough" means that the team accomplishes its goal. Having confidence not in your rightness and perfection but in your ability to select the right people and to motivate them and communicate clearly with them is a hallmark of inclusive leadership. An inclusive leader makes sure that everyone understands where the team and organization want to go. Once the objective is clear to all, an inclusive leader accepts that competent people may find many different ways to get there.

Inclusive leaders are actually curious about these differences. Curiosity leads inclusive leaders to not simply tolerate differences but to actively seek out other perspectives. They are willing to listen to other ideas. They are willing to test other solutions. They are willing to recognize that other ways are sometimes good enough and sometimes even better than "my way." Team learning and process improvements may result. Even if these bonus effects do not occur, the team will accomplish its goals, and team members will be happier and more engaged.

So, if you find yourself in a proverbial kitchen watching someone crack eggs in an unfamiliar way, bite your tongue, accept that there is more than one way to crack an egg, and just enjoy the omelet.

Get Fired Up

Nolan Bushnell, the founder of Atari and Chuck E. Cheese, is quoted as saying: "*Hire for passion and intensity; there is training for everything else.*"

Two truths are evident in this quote: companies typically want people with a passion for the work, and passion cannot easily be taught. Leaders need to understand both of these truths about passion because each of them has important implications for how leaders should work with their teams.

If we are hiring people with passion and intensity for the work, then we should not be surprised when our people show this passion in the workplace. Yet, for a number of reasons, displays of passion destabilize many leaders. Linked closely to the 'my way' bias in Lesson 2, leaders who play their emotional cards close to the vest will expect everyone else to keep calm and carry on. They may find displays of passion odd or unprofessional. Other leaders may not recognize the difference between genuine passion and out-of-control behavior; these leaders will judge emotionally expressive people to be overexcited or even hysterical.

Perhaps, you've been in a meeting where someone is talking eagerly about an idea or an opportunity. Their speech is rapid, and their gestures are animated, but their ideas are clear, and their reasoning is sound. Not understanding that the employee is demonstrating a passion for the work, the boss steps in with a "Calm down!" If you were watching that team member closely, you might have seen their face fall and the flicker of passion extinguish from their eyes.

Turning back to our second truth, passion cannot easily be taught. Leaders who are quick to order a "Calm down" may extinguish the flame of passion. If, as a leader, you extinguish that natural flame, you may never be able to relight it. To avoid snuffing out the flame, leaders must expect their team members to be passionate and allow them to express that passion in their own ways. Leaders also need to learn to observe the difference between excitement and overexcitement in their team members and to make this distinction without judging based on the leader's own pattern of emotional expression. You may be poker-faced by choice or by disposition, but as a leader, you want to allow your followers to show their hands and reveal their passion for the work.

In fact, I'll up the ante and suggest that to be the most effective leader, you need to get fired up yourself. Ample research shows that both positive and negative emotions are contagious in the workplace. People respond positively to the authentic expression of positive emotions, such as by experiencing higher intrinsic motivation, job satisfaction, and engagement.

Your expression of emotion does need to be authentic to have a positive effect. If your natural disposition is cool, calm, and collected, I'm not suggesting that you suddenly pretend to be a cheerleader. You can, however, find ways to show passion for the organization and its mission, the team's projects, and the work and ideas of the people on your team. Positive emotions include not only unbridled happiness but also the emotions of gratitude, pride, interest, amusement, and hope.

Numerous possibilities exist for acknowledging and encouraging passion in your employees and for letting your own positive emotions show. You can avoid premature "calm downs" and allow a team member's passion to shine by expecting and accepting displays of enthusiasm that may be more exuberant than your personal style. A smile, a nod, or a simple and sincere phrase such as, "You've given us some interesting new ideas to consider," can show amusement, appreciation, or interest. As a leader, you can boost team morale and motivate others by showing positive emotions, such as interest in a new idea or gratitude for an employee's contribution or happiness at a team member's success.

Whatever it looks like for you, get fired up!

Don't Stomp Your Feet

If you're the leader and you know it and you really want to show it, what do you do? You don't just clap your hands like the nursery rhyme. Some would-be leaders believe that dramatic displays of authority are necessary to "show 'em who's boss." These people posture like the small child on the playground yelling "Listen to me!" What they do not realize is that demanding that people "respect your authority" has the exact opposite effect. Trying to demonstrate emphatically that you are the boss will put you on the fast track to losing credibility as a leader.

A leader's authority may be based on one or several sources. In more traditional companies or industries, the leader's title alone may give him or her formal authority that employees accept without question. In these cases, the leader should not need to stomp his feet because obedience is automatic; employees who do not get it do not last long. In other organizations, leaders are not necessarily the people at the top; instead, leaders are the people who perform the best or know the most in a particular area. Again, these leaders do not need to stomp their feet because people seek them out for their skill or knowledge.

Problems arise when the source of authority is less clear – either because it is not formally enforced or because it is not generally established. Today, a leader's source of authority is more ambiguous and is often based on the acceptance of the team; they will follow you if they respect you and believe that you have the authority to lead them. Being recognized as the leader is based on a mutual understanding of your position as the leader and their position on the team. The respective roles and responsibilities of a leader and team members also must be clear.

I recall a situation where one of my team members clearly did *not* understand my authority and role as the leader. I had the title of Director at the time, with all the relevant degrees and professional certifications that might signal "authority figure" in the old days. Yet, I received a request from a new hire ranked below me in the official hierarchy. This entry-level employee was asking me to pull reports from a tracking tool that I monitored but that was accessible by everyone in the team, including the new hire. He even indicated exactly how he wanted the reports formatted. I stared at the request, not quite believing what I was reading. I took the opportunity to explain to the new hire how he could obtain the reports himself, hoping the subtle pushback would trigger a realization that his request was inappropriate. Instead, he replied with "Yeah, I'm busy; let me know when the reports are ready."

Once it was clear that *he* was giving *me* an order, I was tempted to go into foot-stamping mode. I could hear the older generation, traditional leaders screaming in my ear: "Does he know who he is talking to? Let this kid know who the boss is!" I was fuming because I thought of all the years I had worked to obtain my Director position only to have a level 1 new hire dare to tell me what to do.

Thankfully, I had observed the evolution of leadership and realized that newer generations do not respond to titles alone. The new hire likely meant no disrespect; he simply did not understand my role or his. I later learned that he was instructed by his own manager to make the misguided request. Thankfully, rather than fire back a stern command that he pull the reports his-doggone-self, I took the time to explain politely but firmly that my role as team leader was to focus on strategic matters and team supervision. I explained that his responsibilities included pulling reports if he thought he needed them and that I could walk him through the process if he was having trouble figuring it out. He not only understood the explanation about this incident, but he got the picture of our respective positions. He pulled those reports and never sent me another request like that again. Taking the time to explain to him our respective roles and responsibilities and to show him that I was willing to teach him had much more of an impact than shouting, "I'm the boss!"

To answer the question I asked earlier, if you're the leader and you know it and you really want to show it, you confirm the team's understanding of your position, you clarify any ambiguities about roles, and you demonstrate your availability to train and support your people. Clarity will also create a culture of accountability within your team as each person knows who is responsible for what. You may need to correct understandings, remind people of responsibilities, and, in some cases, exercise authority through formal discipline.

Unlike the command in the classic song, if you're the leader and you know it and you really want to show it, you do not stomp your feet.

Up or Out

I knew my colleague – I'll call him John – was in trouble as soon as he told me what he'd said to our manager. During his annual review, the manager asked John a standard question: "Where do you want to be in two years?" John responded, "I see myself in your role." In normal circumstances, John's response would have been received as an uncontroversial statement of his desire to advance within the organization. My "uh-oh" reaction was not because of what John said. It was because I knew how our manager would interpret John's statement.

A good leader adopts an "up or out" attitude about his career. An "up or out" attitude focuses on constant growth and professional development. As you acquire knowledge and master skills, you will become good and, perhaps, great at your job. Mastery is certainly an achievement to be celebrated. Stagnation, however, is not (as I'll discuss more in Lesson 6). What I mean is that a good leader intentionally manages his or her career to position themselves for new opportunities either within the company or in a new organization.

An "up or out" focus on your career advancement is not selfish ambition or disloyalty to the organization. As you develop new skills and knowledge for yourself, you are able to contribute to the organization in ways that take full advantage of your talents. You remain engaged, and the company benefits from your continuous improvement. When "up or out" is matched with coaching and mentoring those below you on the ladder, you also contribute to the growth and longevity of the company by developing the people on your teams so that they can move up the ladder as you continue your climb. You train up your people so that one day, they will be able to perform at your level and one day take over your job. Mentoring will benefit the team as you help your people to fulfill their potential and contribute to the team's success. Mentoring can also be personally gratifying as you create your own legacy by leaving behind a number of high-performing professional offspring. Generativity is the opposite of stagnation and has positive emotional benefits; when you focus on developing the next generation in your organization, you make your mark and further your personal growth.

The opposite of "up or out" might be called "stay put." People often get very comfortable in their position and do what is necessary to stay right where they are. They may have achieved mastery and may falsely assume they cannot be as good at doing something else. They may fear the anxiety of learning and not want to go through the discomfort of being a novice again. People may lack imagination or curiosity about new opportunities that would allow them to advance in their careers. In some generations or industries, it is common to plateau in your career; you reach a certain level and set cruise control until you retire. More disturbing reasons for a "stay put" attitude stem from inadequacy or personal insecurities. Some bosses may never have achieved mastery for whatever reason – lack of mentoring, complacency, intellectual limitations – and may feel threatened by those who show the potential to perform their jobs better than they do. Rather than viewing budding rock stars as assets to the team, a leader with a "stay put" attitude will see them as a clear and present danger to the leader's position.

John was either a rock star or a menace, depending on the manager's attitude. Knowing John's manager to be a "stay put" leader, I knew she would interpret his statement to mean, "I'm here to boot you out and take over," and not, "I want to advance in the organization." Her "stay put" attitude, coupled with her own inadequacy, led the manager to want to protect her position at all costs. Rather than developing John and allowing his talents to make the whole team shine, the manager tried to neutralize the perceived personal threat by sabotaging John's work. After a painful 18-month period, John was terminated much to his manager's delight. The story did not, however, end there. Six months later, the manager was terminated. Her incompetence became obvious without stellar team performance to prop her up.

Good leaders invest their energy in developing themselves, not undermining their team members. John's manager might have been better served by focusing on correcting her own professional deficiencies rather than defending her position. The organization certainly would have benefited from her working to level up rather than her scheming to keep John down. When you are focused on the great opportunities that are ahead for you, you are much less concerned about who is behind you in the career advancement line. Instead of seeing them as nipping at your heels, you see talented people as potentially following in your footsteps. Good leaders also invest energy in teaching, providing feedback, coaching, and mentoring their team members. John's manager and the team lost out on the valuable talent and ideas that John was hired to contribute to the company. When you see rock star talent, you inquire about their career ambitions and groom them for the next position, even if it may be yours.

The moral of the story, which John's manager learned the hard way, is look to move up, or you will be moved out.

Be Indispensable, Not Irreplaceable

Harvard Business School professor Amy Edmonson is well-known in academic circles for her work on *psychological safety* in teams. Psychological safety means that teams are safe places for members to speak out, seek help, and make mistakes without the threat of ridicule or exclusion. Consultants and even leaders often seem to forget that the goal is not to create psychological safety simply for safety's sake. In fact, Edmonson's 1999 article that launched the quest to create "safer" teams included two key words in its title – *Learning Behavior*. In a nutshell, Edmonson believed that teams must learn or fail.

The same is true at the individual level. A good leader must loudly and proudly state that she is a "lifelong learner." If you can wear a t-shirt to work, get this phrase printed on one and wear it emblazoned on your chest; if not, change your desk plaque to say, "Jane Q. Leader – Lifelong Learner." Why does this quality merit super-power or official title status?

Being a lifelong learner means having a commitment to continuous learning and professional development. Some people become "experts" at what they do and are happy to have achieved this expert status. They, rightly, derive a good deal of pride from being excellent at something. If they are being honest with themselves, many experts also have to admit that they also derive a great deal of comfort and power from this status. That scary anxiety of learning is a thing of the past, and they have the respect of their peers and subordinates.

Being the resident expert can, however, become dangerous both for you and for the organization.

First, you may be making yourself *irreplaceable*. If you hear the phrase, "No one can do this as well as (insert your name here)" spoken over you frequently, it is very likely that you have become irreplaceable in your current role. While being irreplaceable may sound great, what it means is that you will not have opportunities to move up in the organization. You have been pigeon-holed as the go-to person for unblocking supply chain bottlenecks or for training customer service reps. You are not likely to be considered for any roles that do not require this knowledge if you otherwise have the up-or-out attitude I discussed in Lesson 5.

Another danger of resident "expertitis" is what becomes of the supposedly irreplaceable individual when, suddenly, they are replaced not by another human but by the inexorable march of progress – a new technology disrupts supply chain management or customer service is outsourced to another country. The pigeon-hole and the illusory job security attached to it disappear.

Rather than being content with being an irreplaceable resident expert, leaders must step outside of their comfort zones and ensure that they are up-to-date on the most current industry knowledge and trends. Even with the demands of his former job, President Barack Obama is among the well-respected leaders who consistently dedicate at least five hours per week to deliberate learning. Rather than assuming that they already know everything that they need to know, those who want to progress in an organization position themselves for career-building opportunities by developing knowledge that goes beyond the requirements of their immediate role.

For the organization, the benefits of having leaders who are lifelong learners are invaluable. Lifelong learners view learning as one of the most valuable investments of time. This commitment allows them to take the time to share their knowledge. Lifelong learners do not view teaching as burdensome or knowledge as a rare commodity that must be closely guarded. Instead, they promote a culture of learning in their teams and make professional development a priority for all team members.

Rather than seeking to be irreplaceable in a specific role, lifelong learners become *indispensable* to their organizations. While "irreplaceable" signals limitation, "indispensable" signals possibility. Leaders who are lifelong learners adapt to emerging developments by using new and innovative ideas; they take the initiative by defining and performing the "additional duties required" to fulfill their functions that may not appear on the job description; they grow organizational capability by sharing their knowledge and encouraging learning in their teams. Organizations that want to grow and thrive cannot do without lifelong learner leaders. Make yourself indispensable.

Listen with Your Brain

Stop reading for a second and listen to the sounds around you. Really listen. Do you hear anything you hadn't noticed before? It's possible that sounds have been entering your ears without you paying attention to them. When we give our full attention to the environment around us, our conscious minds pick up on sounds we might have missed with distracted listening.

Hearing (sounds coming into our ears) without listening (sounds registering in and being interpreted by our mind) happens far too often in our interactions with other people. While the other person's voice may be entering our ears, their words are not landing in our brains.

Often, we are listening to respond or defend rather than to understand. While a team member is talking, do you actively run through arguments in your mind, formulating the perfect response? We all can be guilty of this at times. Even if you think you know the other person like a book, any response developed without actually listening to what the other person is saying in that moment will not be perfect. Your response will likely ignore any subtleties the speaker introduced and any feelings the speaker displayed. So many misunderstandings and conflicts arise simply because we do not pick up on the other person's cues that allow us to have a deeper understanding of what their words mean. The slight pause, the sigh, the higher pitch to the voice, the unusual word choice or turn of phrase – any of these might say, "Don't take my words at face value."

Distracted listening has an antidote. The cure is to make a conscious choice to engage in active listening. Active listening is a communication skill that requires the listener to give his or her full attention to the speaker. Just like you concentrated on those sounds in your environment at the start of this chapter, in your conversations with other people, you fully concentrate on the speaker, their words, their non-verbal cues (facial expressions and posture), and their feelings. Once you're a skilled active listener, you can even develop an awareness of the energy in the room and what is not being said out loud. This skill requires ignoring your own thoughts while the other person is speaking so that the full attention of your active mind is squarely on the speaker.

Active listening also requires interpreting all the information you have gathered through observation and seeking to understand what is really being said. Only *after* you have observed and understood do you respond. A response to what is really being said in the present conversation will be much closer to perfect than a response crafted based on what *might* have been said or what is *usually* said. Observation is better than imagination or presumption.

When a leader does not practice active listening in the workplace, the consequences for the team and the organization are both human and operational.

The **human cost** of bad listening is in missed opportunities to connect with team members. In work, as in life, when people feel truly heard and understood, they feel more valued. Team members who feel that they matter are more committed to the team and the organization. A little focused attention goes a long way toward boosting morale, motivation, performance, and cohesiveness.

The **operational cost** of bad listening is in time-wasting do-overs or, worse, unfixable mistakes. When leaders do not hear the specifications, concerns, and reservations of team members, valuable input into projects is ignored. Teams may perform tasks that are unnecessary or perform necessary tasks in the wrong way. Teams may plow ahead with a course of action that is doomed to fail. Leaders may delegate overly complex jobs to people who have subtly signaled that they are unwilling or unable to live up to the challenge.

Active listening is a competence that must be developed by constant practice. Every leader has different tactics for active listening. Personally, I sit on my hands or grasp them in front of me to remind me that it is not my turn to talk. As someone who talks using a lot of gestures, if my hands are not free to jump into action, I am more likely to concentrate fully on what is being said. Another tactic is to keep your mouth shut, meaning physical feeling your lips together. Other leaders put visible reminders in their field of vision, such as a Post-It note with "LISTEN!" written on it or more subtle suggestions, such as a drawing of an ear or the third-eye. Some silence potential distractions, including the constant ding of incoming e-mails, by putting their phones in their desks, turning off their computers, or meeting with people in a small conference room.

Other tactics include setting up the room so that the speaker has your full attention. Move chairs around so that you can have appropriate eye contact with the other person. Looking the other person in the eye signals that you are listening and can also help you to notice facial expressions that might be helpful in understanding what is really being said. Eye contact does not, however, mean that you are having a staring contest, and it is important to be sensitive to individual and cultural variations on how comfortable people are with eye contact. While Americans may interpret a lack of eye contact as a signal of deceit or untrustworthiness, in other cultures, prolonged direct eye contact is perceived as threatening, sexually provocative, or simply unacceptable. Some individuals may break eye contact to think more deeply about a point, as they imagine scenarios in their mind. Learn about individuals and use eye contact to connect in a way that is comfortable for each team member. If you cannot figure out what is going on, it's okay to ask.

To respond based on what has really been said, there may be a lag time while your mind processes all the cues you have observed. It is okay not to respond in the split second when the other person stops speaking. Unfortunately, many people are uncomfortable with silence and fill the void with imperfect noise. Become comfortable with not having a ready answer by saying, "Let me think about that" and by sitting in silence in the presence of another person.

Active listening will raise the level of conversation and connection within teams and organizations, and, in the long run, it will save everyone's time.

Listen not with your ears but with your brain.

Reach Out

"Good leaders keep it professional, and only professional." I received this advice early in my career from a manager I'll call Kate. Kate was telling me not to get too close to my employees and, in fact, to maintain a strict separation between work life and personal life. She was essentially telling me not to reveal much, if anything, about myself and also not to inquire about my employees. Kate meant well, but, in my experience, she was dead wrong.

I discovered the truth for myself not as a result of deliberate disobedience to Kate but because my personality pulls me toward other people. I found myself naturally in conversations that ranged freely into the personal topics of family or weekend plans. When I heard Kate's voice echoing in my ears telling me to put an abrupt end to these not-purely-professional discussions, I ignored it, and an amazing thing happened. My effectiveness as a leader actually improved because I was better able to gauge how to manage my employees.

Learning about your team members not only professionally but also personally helps you to understand what makes them "tick." Learning details of people's personal lives allowed me to know why they got up in the morning and chose to come to work – what motivated them to do their jobs. Seek to know their likes, dislikes, motivators, distractors, goals, and objectives. When you have a better understanding of their hopes and dreams and fears, you can activate their drive and alleviate their concerns in more individualized ways.

To be clear, I am not suggesting that leaders need to know everything about their team members or to hang out as buddies every weekend. We do, however, spend almost half of our waking time with our colleagues and, during those almost 2,100 hours of togetherness per year, employees value having a leader who demonstrates some concern for their well-being. Keeping it professional, and professional only, will not show employees that you care.

Reach out beyond the professional boundaries to begin to find out about your team as people with lives outside the office. Start simply by asking employees, "How are you?" and then, really, *actively* listen to their responses. The phrase, "I'm fine" has almost as many interpretations as that old Southern favorite, "Bless your heart." You may hear enthusiasm or demotivation or frustration or hope. Sometimes, just following up with a sincere "Yeah?" or "Really?" or, "You're fine?" may create space for the employee to express how they really are.

You will have more context to interpret those two loaded words if you actually know a bit about the person. You do not need or want to pry to discover personal stories. You can model self-disclosure by sharing your own stories with your employees. Leading by example signals to the team that it is okay for them to talk about personal topics, and it also gives an indication of the appropriate tone and scope of these discussions. While I am eager and interested in knowing employees as people, some language is not appropriate for the office. Respectful discussion without cursing or colorful stories will maintain the right amount of professionalism and keep your human resources department happy.

I mention HR because in reaching out to your employees, it is possible, and perhaps inevitable, that some will share personal details that are sensitive and beyond your capacity to deal with as a manager. This inevitability probably gets to the real reason for Kate's line in the sand about professional boundaries. As leaders, we often discover painful details of our employees' lives over which we have zero control but that 100% affect their state of mind at work. More than creating discomfort, this awareness can make a leader feel powerless.

Rather than ignoring personal issues to avoid these unpleasant feelings, effective leaders must keep an eye on employees even when the leader cannot individually resolve the employees' issues. Referring employees with sensitive personal struggles to an HR support officer or the appropriate service in your organization allows employees to find the right resources to address their difficulties and to get their head back in the game at work.

Kate may also have maintained her line because she saw others or experienced being taken advantage of by employees. Every organization has the insincere, long-suffering person who raises all their personal issues solely to gain special treatment. They essentially manipulate the perceived kindness of their leader to have an easier time at work. Learning to recognize people with these tendencies during the intake process can spare the organization the toxic consequences of their behavior. If a manipulator does slip in the door, the minute you realize what's going on, speak up and nip it in the bud – *"Isn't this the third time your grandmother died?"* You can also enact strategies to minimize the risk of manipulation, such as having clear rules about extraordinary absences or other special accommodations.

Finding the right balance between individualized concern and over-personalization of the workplace is a necessary but worthwhile challenge that comes with erasing Kate's line in the sand. Shutting everyone out because of a few bad apples cuts the leader off from valuable information about the team and from opportunities to be a better leader.

Leaders who understand that the personal effects the professional take care of their teams. This care and consideration are hallmarks of authentic leadership, which I use to mean a leadership style focused on being genuine and leading with both the head and the heart. An authentic leadership style builds trust with followers, which, in turn, drives employee motivation. Authentic leaders are more likable and connected to their employees but remain mission-driven and focused on results.

You can care about the business *and* about the people. Reach out and learn about the amazing people who are your colleagues.

What Do You Say? Hint: Just a smidge of gratitude.

Many parents instantly recognize the question, "What do you say?" as the phrase you repeat multiple times a day to prompt your children to say, "Thank you." Yet, despite this parental investment in teaching manners, saying a spontaneous "Thank you" seems to be less and less common.

Much has been written about whether the present society and the most recent generation of people entering the workforce are entitled and ungrateful. The current ethos is a topic for another book, but let's consider "thank you" in the business context.

I have observed the art of saying "thank you" become rarer and rarer as the workplace evolves. In an increasingly fast-paced world, we race to respond to unending emails and to meet outrageous deadlines. When we succeed in satisfying all the demands of our work, the reward is often more email and tighter deadlines. Our attention is consumed by laptops, phones, and tablets. Rarely does anyone pause to celebrate success and acknowledge the hard work of the team.

One manager insisted that there is no need to "thank people for doing what is supposed to be their job." Other managers say, "A paycheck is thanks enough." Both of these attitudes make me cringe. This can create a culture of employees saying, "I'm just doing my job."

Thanking people who go beyond their job requirements certainly makes sense. In today's more fluid work environment, a number of people are performing tasks that are not strictly in their job descriptions. Remembering to thank them will reward their initiative, and a public thanks may encourage others to make similar efforts.

But are we simply to ignore the efforts of people who perform their job requirements in extraordinary ways? The rock star who does "what is supposed to be their job" in an impressive fashion. The person who fulfills their stated job requirements in such an efficient manner that it saves the company money or wins the team praise. Certainly, these "just doing their job" performers also deserve some thanks. When so many people are content doing the bare minimum required, leaders can reinforce desirable behaviors and levels of performance by giving recognition to those who perform their jobs well.

If the monthly paycheck or a bonus is the only form of appreciation, people will feel more appreciated by a company that pays more. An employee will remain loyal only as long as the price is right. They may even jump ship for a company that pays exactly the same amount but where the managers actually take time to say thanks. Verbal expressions of appreciation and other non-monetary forms of encouragement have been shown, in certain circumstances, to be more motivating than money. Like listening and inquiring, which I discussed in previous lessons, showing appreciation in the workplace increases trust between leaders and team members.

So many ways to show appreciation exist that one is certain to fit your personal style. You can say "Thank you" face-to-face or send an encouraging email or even leave a Post-It on a file or on the person's computer screen. Saying "Thanks" or "Way to go" or "Great job" lifts employees' moods by releasing endorphins. These happy hormones create a positive feeling in the body and motivate employees even in the hardest of times. Rather than racing blindly from deadline to deadline and risking burn-out, employees who are offered an appreciative pause are able to refresh their energy and attention, boosting morale and productivity.

Don't wait for a parent to ask the eternal question; instead, spontaneously make time to show appreciation for a task well done. Show a smidge of gratitude.

Fight the Good Fight

"I don't like conflict."

Leaders who make this statement are really saying, "I avoid conflict." Few, if any, people actually *like* conflict, but leaders must face conflict head-on, whether they like it or not.

A leader who allows his or her dislike of conflict to become a reason to avoid addressing it allows the conflict to take root and fester. Controlled, facilitated conflict can be a great tool to "mine for conflict." This can be done through the concept of "roses and thorns." As a leader, you want to hear the good and bad. However, unresolved conflict has hard costs and soft costs for an organization. When a team leader ignores the root of the conflict and attempts to address only the symptoms, he is putting expensive but ineffective Band-Aids on a gaping wound. In the classic sitcom, *The Office*, rather than firing an underperforming manager and promoting the talented salesperson, the company decided to create "co-manager" positions. Neither person was completely happy, and the employees were confused about who was in charge of what. Equally ridiculous situations occur every day in real companies. These quick fixes cost the company money to implement and result in losses of productivity.

The principal soft cost of unresolved conflict is sinking team morale. The conflict will either create a persistent unease or, worse, escalate creating a hole that becomes deeper and harder to climb out of the longer the conflict goes on. People will leave, and you, as a leader, will lose credibility and trust.

Again, whether you like it or not, to be an effective leader, you must not turn a blind eye to conflict in your team. Identify it and address it by talking to the people involved. Staying factual and avoiding forming any opinion or listening to hearsay helps to discuss the conflict in a way that does not add fuel to the flame. Leaders should avoid emotions or accusations and try to understand the behavior and triggers that are causing the employees to be in conflict. Writing a script for these conversations can help you stay focused on the facts, the topic, and remove emotion.

Stepping into a conflict between team members or creating a conflict by confronting a team member will expose you, as a leader, to potential hostility. Nobody likes conflict, remember? When they can no longer flee, employees may switch into fight mode. To achieve your ultimate goal of removing the conflict, you, as leader, must be prepared for what might come back at you. Employees may accuse you of being an ineffective leader – *"We wouldn't have this problem if you were doing your job!"*

Self-awareness is essential to avoid being drawn into a secondary conflict, one that is not the real issue that needs to be resolved. You will need to understand your conflict-handling style, your triggers, and your behaviors when you are attacked. You will want to be open to receiving criticism, even if it is not phrased in the most professional way. You will want to remain professional, kind, and focused on the real conflict. You will want to be willing to gain clarity about what the real conflict actually is.

If you are able to be socially aware and self-aware, to remain factual and professional, and to keep the focus on the goal of restoring harmony, trust, and productivity to the workplace, you will be fighting the good fight.

Bad fights can be avoided by fighting the good fight early.

No Capes Required

For much of human history, whether in leadership, literature, or in the popular imagination, the leader was cast as a "great man" with extraordinary, God-given attributes. These great men were supposedly born to lead and had a distinctive air about them that set them apart from ordinary people. They were seen as capable of performing astounding feats even when the odds were stacked against them. They saved the day, or the company, or the nation, or even the world. In short, leaders were superheroes.

Even though leadership theory has officially moved away from this antiquated view, the "leader as superhero" myth lingers. We often have unrealistic expectations of leaders, believing not only that they are special but that they are perfect. No leader that you have had, that you currently have, or that you will have in the future knows everything there is to know about leadership, managing people, or managing business. Leaders are human.

As a leader, you need to be aware that your team members will be inclined to place you on a pedestal, but you need to understand that is it is not about YOU. Knowing about this tendency for followers to idealize their leader can help you to disrupt potentially dysfunctional dynamics. When a leader is viewed as a superhero, this idealization creates two perverse effects: the followers are not empowered to reach their full potential, and that leader is not allowed to be his unique self.

Think about those scenes from your favorite superhero flick where everyone is desperately asking, "Where is our saving hero?" Maybe it's the people of Metropolis feeling helpless until Superman flies in to save the day or the police force in Gotham wondering how crime got so out of control since Batman abandoned the city or even the fierce female soldiers of Wakanda fighting every fiber in their being to pledge loyalty to Killmonger until the good and true King T'Challa is resurrected. What all these scenes have in common is the sense of helplessness and pending destruction and doom that can only be dispelled by the superhero leader.

While these circumstances make for great movie drama, a similar sense of dependency and confusion within an organization can lead to disaster. If the leader is viewed as the only one capable of solving problems, organizational challenges that fall outside the leader's human competencies may be insurmountable. Additionally, the failure to empower people at all levels within the organization will lead to dissatisfaction and departures of the most desirable employees. People who want to contribute their ideas, energy, and intelligence to the organization – the best and the brightest – will be frustrated by the reactive, lethargic atmosphere that comes with waiting for solutions from above. To create a proactive, enthusiastic dynamic within the team and organization, the leader must share the power and lose the cape.

Speaking of capes, if we think about superheroes, they often wear disguises or have alter-egos, living in fear that their powers will one day be revealed. This double-life is a source of sometimes comic anxiety, but if we look more deeply, we see that it often creates a sense of loneliness for the superhero. He relates to most people in an inauthentic way and is able to connect completely only with the few who know his true identity. When a leader accepts being treated as a superhero, he also agrees to show followers only a perfect and perfectly false version of who he is.

Maintaining the superhero façade harms both the quality of relationships with followers and the leader's self-awareness. Projecting fakeness creates distance in relationships, and in the leadership context, this distance makes it difficult to establish trust. As I've explained in prior chapters, trust is essential to effective leadership because it increases many performance-boosting attitudes: commitment, job satisfaction, engagement, and sense of meaningfulness. For the leader, pretending to be perfect may lead to feeling perfect. The pedestal may begin to feel not only comfortable but well-deserved. If the leader begins to internalize his idealized image, self-awareness and humility are sacrificed. All those warts I discussed in Chapter 1 become "beauty marks," and the leader feels no need to address his shortcomings and weaknesses.

The superhero myth creates isolated, overconfident leaders. Leaders must retire their capes and embrace their humanity.

Four Simple Words

Learn to say the following words: "I made a mistake." Lather, rinse, and repeat until the words flow easily and naturally.

A leader should never pretend that he or she did not make a mistake. As I discussed in Chapter 11, effective leaders do not pretend to be perfect. One way to dispel the superhero myth and to reshape follower expectations is to admit when you have made a mistake.

Our mistakes do not necessarily define us. Well-meaning people make bad decisions. They botch the job. They disappoint others. Even the best leaders make mistakes. None of these blunders makes them bad people or bad leaders. If you are stretching and growing and taking on new roles and responsibilities, the likelihood of making mistakes is even higher. The more you move out of your comfort zone and adopt an "up or out" mentality, the harder it will be to avoid mistakes. And that's okay.

What defines us is not our mistakes but how we respond to them. Acknowledging a mistake is a sign of strength and communicates that you are human. I have learned that when you make a mistake, you should do only three things next: admit it, learn from it, and do not repeat it.

Once the mistake has been made, the team can either look back or look forward. Looking back involves searching for the culprit – who messed up? This blame game shifts the team into battle mode, with each person trying to justify his decisions or emphasize his individual performance. Rather than focusing on the team's task or the organization's mission, people use energy defending their reputations or honor. The sooner the person who made the mistake admits it, the sooner the team can move out of battle mode and into solution mode.

On an interpersonal level, admitting mistakes opens space for grace. When you make a mistake and admit it quickly, you will trigger more positive reactions than if you wait for it to blow over or, worse, cover it up. Think about the last time someone admitted a mistake to you. It is disarming in the literal sense of the word; the person who confesses takes the weapons out of your hands. Once you get over your astonishment that the person actually fessed up, your confusion and anger disappear. You move out of attack and punish mode. Instead, you want to reward the person's courage and honesty by showing mercy and working together to find a fix.

Having the ability to admit your mistakes as a leader will humanize you and create more harmonious team dynamics.

But don't use these four simple words as a sort of "get out jail free card." Remember that along with admitting mistakes, you also need to learn from them and not repeat them. If you commit the same mistake over and over and hope an "Oops, my bad" will resolve the situation each time, you will soon learn that few people are willing or able to forgive seventy times seven as a wise man once commanded.

You would do well to learn the lesson and eliminate the mistake quickly.

When it comes to success, it's not the number of mistakes you make; it's the number of times you make the same mistake.

Admit, learn, do not repeat.

Speak Up. Use Your Voice.

Several years ago, I worked in an organization that put on a good show when it came to diversity and inclusion. They promoted minorities, including me, into leadership positions. On the surface, it seemed that the organization valued minority voices and perspectives.

The opposite was, in fact, accurate. It was a *Human Resource Compliance* "Check The Box." The real reason the organization placed so many minorities in leadership positions was to comply with Department of Labor guidelines. They did not value or even desire input from these "check-the-box" leaders. Our pretty titles were awarded as meaningless tokens-with little authority to manage or lead, think or even talk.

Little did the organization know that I was going to leverage my title. Even though I had been invited to the table apparently to satisfy the Department of Labor, I knew I had worked hard to earn my seat. Whatever the organization's motivations, I knew that I deserved the title. So, I refused to remain silent and treated my title with all the seriousness it should have conveyed. Even when colleagues wanted to view me as a "token" promotion, I continued to speak up until they realized that I had valid ideas, that my contributions were more than worthy of the pretty title.

I learned from this experience that however you get your seat at the table, you must use it. Do not sit silently even when others want to silence you. Do not be afraid to express your thoughts and opinions even when others may doubt their significance. Once you have that seat at the table, make sure that you are heard and eventually respected and even welcome.

Using your voice will ensure that you are heard. Using your voice *strategically* will help you to gain respect. Strategic contributions add value to the discussion; use your voice to advocate for choices that move the group in the direction of organizational goals. Strategic contributions should be inclusive; use your voice to amplify important perspectives that may be overlooked and to find common ground. Strategic contributions reflect calculated risk-taking; use your voice to promote reasonable investigation of alternatives and bold choices based on reliable information. Strategic contributions are carefully timed and crafted; listen to what others are saying and not saying and choose your words wisely.

Strong and strategic voices may not always be welcome, but once those around the table recognize how your presence improves the process and the decisions, they will wonder how they functioned without you.

If you find yourself at the table with a group that does not respect or welcome your strategic contributions even after a reasonable period of adjustment, two explanations are possible: either your contributions are not as valuable as you think, or the group is simply incapable of seeing the value of your contributions.

In some situations, you may take your seat and realize that you need to spend some time understanding the organization and its objectives. If you begin contributing without taking the time to get the lay of the land, you may erode your credibility, which will be difficult to rebuild. Self-awareness will help you determine whether you make yourself heard with opinions or with intelligent inquiries. Either way, you should not remain silent.

In some situations, the group may suffer from some dysfunction that makes it unlikely that good contributions will be appreciated. A committee that actually desires to do as little as possible or a board that prefers false harmony to constructive conflict will see voices for change or bold action as disruptive or dangerous. Continue to use your seat at the table unless and until it becomes obvious that you are crying into the wind.

Always try to make yourself heard. You will not win every battle for respect and acceptance, but always use your voice. Speak up.

Avoid Creating Wallflowers or Benchwarmers

A few years ago, the human resources director asked me if I thought our organization was diverse. My immediate response was "Absolutely!" I then paused, waiting for her to ask me what I thought was an obvious follow-up question. She never did.

I do not know if she already knew my answer would be "no" or if the question was not obvious to her, but I expected her to ask, "Do you think we are inclusive?" She did not.

We *were* diverse; we had employees of a variety of races, genders, sexual identities, world views, religions, work experiences, backgrounds, and the list goes on. Yet, sadly, like many other organizations, we did not take care to include all of these people when seeking opinions, making decisions, or designing and implementing projects – the inclusive piece. The decision-makers were all the same, the "usual suspects." To paraphrase Verna Myers, the organization had invited a diverse group of people to the party, but the leaders did not ask all of their employees to dance. Instead, people of diverse backgrounds stood on the fringes of decision-making like wallflowers ignored at the prom.

Early in my career, I did not understand how diversity and inclusion was an important aspects of organizational culture. I blame youth and ignorance. As I grew in my career and had the opportunity to work in more senior roles, however, I started to look around and noticed that there were not many people who looked "like me," especially in the management levels. As I learned more about "Diversity" and "Inclusion" and the difference between the two concepts, I realized that both of these aspects are equally important. Many organizations get the diversity piece right, but they do not encourage inclusion. Making inclusion a priority ensures that all human talent, as unique as they are, is not only present but actually represented.

Improving inclusion in organizations demands investment at both the organizational and the personal level.

Organizations and their collective leadership must assess their efforts to foster progress. Committing to diversity and inclusion improves the work environment and allows organizations to gain a lasting competitive advantage. Unlike sports teams, business organizations do not have the luxury of having backup players. Every employee must be allowed and encouraged to contribute fully. When organizations review their diversity and inclusion efforts with attention to details beyond the raw numbers on diversity, they can gain greater clarity about what's missing from their inclusion efforts. Is the organization seeking to build capabilities throughout the organization by understanding how diversity and inclusion influences employee engagement and interpersonal relationships? Looking at what positions and levels of responsibility diverse employees hold and what voices are missing from decision-making can help organizations to see whether they have a fully engaged team or a group of benchwarmers that the organizational leadership or culture has sidelined.

At the level of individual leaders, inclusion requires a willingness to move beyond the traditional or easy way of doing things and an ability to accept the discomfort that comes with change. "Tradition" and "ease" are often buzzwords that maintain the status quo about who should be consulted and who can be left out. These *shoulds* are social norms that many people have absorbed because of their experiences. In this way, they are often the result of implicit or unconscious biases. To begin to be more inclusive, leaders must understand when their unconscious biases come into play. Understanding whose voices you value (or undervalue) and why you view them that way is one of the defining aspects of the radical self-awareness that I spoke about in Chapter 1.

Rather than promoting their own ease and comfort, inclusive leaders ask, "How can I make the work environment comfortable and safe for everyone to be his or her authentic self?" Inclusive leaders understand how organizational structures or unspoken cultural norms may force some employees to try to fit in or pretend to be "just like" the faces they see in leadership. Inclusive leaders check these expectations and allow all employees to be themselves. Because of the leader's openness, patience, empathy, and genuine interest in people, employees get the message, "You can be who you are."

Inclusive leadership is not to be confused with a laissez-faire or make-nice attitude. Inclusive leaders do set and enforce the boundaries of good organizational functioning. They do not use employees' diversity to excuse unprofessional behaviors, such as lateness, rudeness, or sloppiness; instead, they tap employees' unique talents and motivations to empower the employees to bring their best selves to work. Inclusive leaders also foster healthy difference. They do not insist on superficial harmony; instead, they mine for constructive conflict – roses and thorns.

An inclusive leadership culture will hasten and sustain a diverse workplace. It attracts diverse candidates and promotes retention of diverse employees. These dynamics, in turn, create a competitive advantage for the organization as well as high team morale, trust, and efficiency. Organizations must not only invest in inclusive leadership but also promote it and encourage it.

As a leader committed to organizational performance, you need to practice inclusive leadership. Whether you prefer the prom or the sports team metaphor, you need to look around and see who is just waiting for a chance to show off their moves on the floor or the field.

The "So, What?" Question

A Chinese proverb often attributed to the great and wise Confucius states, "The man who asks a question is a fool for a minute; the man who does not ask is a fool for life."

I have been criticized for asking too many questions. Perhaps I was perceived as needing too much explanation or detail or not trusting my team or, in a word, micromanaging. So, I took the hint and stopped asking questions, trusting that people would work out the reasons and objectives for doing things and anticipate the necessary planning for projects to be successful. You can guess what happened next. The questions did not get asked by me or anyone else, and I was criticized for not asking enough questions.

Like Goldilocks with her bed and her porridge, I had to find the "just right" solution. My happy medium for asking questions is to ask one simple question, sometimes repeatedly. Some of the most effective decision-making coaching sessions drill down to the heart of the client's dilemma by repeating, "Why is that important?" until the client finds the true purpose for wanting to do or to avoid doing something – one simple question, "So, what?"

Rather than using it as a brusque criticism that what the other person has said is unimportant, I use "So, what?" as a respectful invitation for the person to explain to me why their idea, plan, or project *is* important. Because I care about the proposal or the work my team member is discussing, I ask this question as many times as necessary to trigger critical thinking. Moving forward without thinking critically about a decision can lead to expensive consequences in companies. Rushed decisions may be based on incomplete information, erroneous assumptions, or irrational factors, such as fear or misplaced enthusiasm.

Critical thinking can be an antidote as it involves basing decisions on adequate information, careful analysis, and coherent reasoning. I have seen critical thinking improve decision-making and problem-solving. Asking "So, what?" invites the person to think about whether they have all the data necessary or whether additional investigation might be required. Asking "So, what?" forces the person to question whether all of their assumptions are sound or whether they might need to be revised or updated. Asking "So, what?" challenges the person to provide justifications based on objective factors instead of emotion. Many of my team's projects have been successful because critical thinking allowed us to dive deeper into the situation or problem. We were able to avoid pitfalls and to anticipate obstacles.

Triggering critical thinking among your team members will also increase intellectual stimulation, a key factor in employee engagement. Helping people to solve problems more creatively and skillfully has been shown to boost employees' commitment and effort.

Beyond these team member and organizational benefits, the leader will also benefit professionally from asking the question, "So, what?" You will develop a better understanding of the project and potential challenges by asking team members to share their reflections. In resolving conflicts between team members, asking, "So, what?" allows you to gain perspective on the different values, viewpoints, and concerns that may be at play. This enhanced insight will allow you to gain clarity and insight into where your involvement is needed and into how best to contribute your knowledge and skills to the success of the project or the resolution of the problem. Rather than basing your input or actions on your own assumptions about what will work, you will be able to tailor your involvement to the specific circumstances and, in doing so, increase your repertoire of leadership interventions. Asking, "So, what?" can help you advance in your leadership development and your career.

Taking time to ask questions for clarity – not as a personal challenge or a questioning of someone's integrity – means that better decisions will be made and, in most cases, better outcomes will be achieved.

So, what are you going to ask next time a team member comes to you with an idea, plan, or problem? "So, what?"

Choose Your Words Carefully

Words have power. Words spoken verbally in a meeting, words written in an e-mail, even words thought silently to ourselves. The words we use shape our lives and the lives of others, often in irreversible ways.

If we observe children on a playground, it is almost inevitable that one will insult another. The insulted child's defensive response will often be, "Take that back," as though a retraction will lessen the sting of the insult. As adults, we have to realize that words communicated carelessly cannot be taken back easily. Even if we do have the opportunity to walk back or correct our comments, the hurt will likely linger long after the hurtful words have been made to disappear.

In the workplace, words spoken or written in haste may have career-ending consequences, costly organizational consequences, or embarrassing legal consequences. Leaders do not have the luxury of saying things that they might later regret. As a leader, you must choose your words carefully.

Choosing carefully the words that you use for others requires paying attention to the words, the timing, and the audience.

Some words are always off-limits and should never be used in an organizational context. Offensive terms, such as slurs based on race, gender, or sexual identity or vulgar words have no place in the workplace. You may think that you are just joking around with your buddies or blowing off some steam with trusted associates, but those ugly words can and will be used against you in an office power struggle. Choosing the right words means removing some words from your professional vocabulary.

The right words spoken at the wrong time can also create a negative atmosphere. If your words do not match the mood of the group, you may inadvertently signal to people that they do not matter. For example, an ill-timed joke will not only go over like a lead balloon, but it may also convey to the person speaking that their issue is not being taken seriously. Similarly, as I mentioned in Lesson 3, downer words when the group is feeling passionate and inspired will dampen the collective spirit. Even words intended to provide individual motivation can come across as insults if, from the employee's perspective, it is a lack of organizational resources or leader support and not their own effort or attitude that is the primary problem. Finally, a person may simply not be ready to hear the words at the time that you want to speak them. Asking whether the person is receptive to the message will avoid wasted words and frustrating repetition. Choosing the right words requires understanding the specific circumstances and using appropriate words for the moment or waiting for a better moment.

The listener's expectations will also greatly influence how words are received. We craft messages in our minds, often picking words based on our own sensibilities and perspectives. We often forget that those words will be interpreted in the mind of the listener using their sensibilities and perspectives, not ours. The possibility of a gap between the intended message and the perceived message is, therefore, substantial. We can reduce this gap by anticipating the other person's feelings and perceptions and framing the message in words that are meaningful to them. Adapting your language to the person on the receiving end will help ensure that the words are not hurtful and that the message will be interpreted more accurately. Choosing the right words involves matching your words to your audience.

I recall a leader pulling me aside just after I had delivered a report to the board. He said, "You did not sound as peppy as you normally do. The words you used didn't sound peppy." In addition to the implicit insult of having my contribution judged based solely on whether I sounded bouncy and vibrant despite my 20 years of professional experience (wrong audience), his words were inappropriate because the news we had just delivered to the board was not good (wrong timing). The leader could have reframed his real message by saying, "The board report should have been focused more on future opportunities than on recent challenges." I would have received this statement as an invitation to engage and discuss proper strategy and, perhaps, ethics for reporting and oversight. Instead, I was left with the impression that my sole value in his eyes was as a cheerleader or propagandist.

When I choose my words as a leader, in addition to paying attention to the situation and the person, I pay attention to myself, my tone, and my body language. This self-examination begins with making sure that the words that occupy my free attention are affirming words. Millions of words and thoughts automatically and spontaneously pass through our minds, but we have control over those that catch and hold our attention. I choose words that will shape my own mind in positive ways. When I am using words with others, I examine my own motives. Before opening my mouth or pulling up to my keyboard, I seek to answer two questions: "Why am I saying this?" and "How will this statement serve me?" If I do not have a clear answer to these questions, or if the answer is that the words will be self-motived, I re-examine and revise until my words can be motivated by team or organizational objectives. As a leader, speaking from a pure heart will improve your ability to choose the right words.

Right vocabulary, right time, right viewpoint, right intention – the complete ingredient list for carefully choosing the right words.

The Power of the Pause

Noise surrounds us everywhere in modern life. Whether it's the sounds of traffic, the humming of household machines, or the person screaming into their cell phone in a public space, this constant noise makes silence all the more surprising and powerful. Even in situations where continuous talking is expected, silence can have a dramatic impact. I call this impact "the power of the pause."

The most effective professors and trainers know that the power of the pause will allow students to digest their material more completely. The most effective public speakers know that the power of the pause will add depth and intrigue to the narrative they are developing. The best face-to-face communicators know that the power of the pause will allow them to establish a better connection with the other person; the pause avoids misunderstandings by allowing the other person to process the message more deliberately and accurately and to ask clarifying questions.

One manager I encountered did not recognize the power of the pause. He would talk and talk and talk and... well, you get it. I recall one meeting where he intended to provide corrective feedback to a colleague and me. The meeting lasted for 42 minutes, and our manager talked for exactly 37 of those 42 minutes, without pausing. He never allowed my colleague and me an opportunity to rebut his criticisms, defend against his accusations, or ask questions to clarify the proposed remedies to our underperformance. We left the meeting literally dazed and confused with no clear understanding of the situation or of how to resolve it. Instead of receiving usable corrective feedback, we felt that we had just been scolded.

This experience permitted me to see how leader monologues affect followers. We did not feel empowered to ask questions or propose our own solutions. We did not feel encouraged to contribute value to the so-called conversation because it was a one-way stream of communication. And after numerous prior experiences of this manager babbling on and on, we did not feel engaged to listen after the first few minutes; we understood that the content would be repetitive and that he did not expect any response. The monologue (or diatribe) model of leadership communication creates disempowered, discouraged, and disengaged followers.

Leaders who use the power of the pause create space for followers to demonstrate their own knowledge, to express their concerns, and to contribute or analyze their valuable ideas. These leaders use the pause as a silent invitation for others to engage in conversation. The pause indicates that the leader values others' ideas and input. The pause allows for team collaboration by allowing team members to step up and step in during the silence. The pause models for team members that silent reflection is often more valuable than heaping up meaningless words.

To channel the power of the pause, leaders must be self-confident. Standing in front of a room in total silence can be a scary experience. The intimacy of sitting in silence with another person also has the potential to create anxiety. Many leaders will "just keep talking" for fear of being asked a difficult question or being told a difficult truth. A self-confident leader is not afraid of silence or of what may come when he or she stops talking, giving others permission to speak.

To use the power of the pause effectively, leaders also need to be emotionally intelligent. As with choosing the right words, timing is essential when using silence. As a leader, if you are aware of your audience, you can pick the moments when the pause will have the most power. Know when energy is peaking and your audience needs relief from the emotional high that you've created with your words; know when a person is on the verge of an insight that just a few more seconds of silence will allow.

Emotional intelligence and awareness of the audience will also allow you to know when the pause might be inappropriate; the audience may experience it like a song ending abruptly as though the power was cut off. Pausing simply to create interest in an uninteresting narrative or to stall for time because you are unprepared would be an abuse of the power. The pause should be used responsibly and not in a way that creates anxiety, frustration, or confusion.

Learning to use the power of the pause is a necessary leadership skill to show your people that you are interested in them and to get their best contributions.

The next time you are speaking to others, please press pause.

Watch Your Back

U nfortunately, not everyone you encounter in the course of your career will be rooting for you.

One of the important lessons that my mother shared with me was simple: You will meet people who simply do not like you. Through no act or fault of your own, it will appear as though these people invest their energy in despising you. In middle school, it was probably for childish reasons. As an adult, and particularly in the workplace, it is for more complex reasons, but it is equally confusing and unfortunate. Once you accept this unsavory truth, it is easier to protect yourself from the haters. You will recognize them more quickly and easily. You will create boundaries to neutralize them or develop strategies to avoid them. You will be able to nurture your self-esteem by distinguishing constructive criticism from comments intended to drag you down. Understanding that some people will not like you for reasons you cannot change (and that usually have nothing to do with you) frees you to remain uninjured by their behaviors.

Accepting the existence of irrational haters is difficult, but experiencing the reality of backstabbers is even harder. One of the most painful lessons I had to learn to grow as a leader is that the people who have a leadership responsibility to help you develop do not always have your best interests at heart.

I am not speaking about those who might have a legitimate ax to grind for one reason or another. You may, for example, have engaged in some questionable political maneuvering that rubbed your boss the wrong way; you may have failed to deliver on a promise or a project that had big consequences for the team and the organizations' leaders. It would hardly be surprising when these people begin to take actions designed to undermine you.

When I refer to backstabbers, I am speaking about supervisors or managers who give every signal that they are invested in your professional growth. It comes as a painful shock when one of these seemingly trusted advisors fails to look out for you or even blocks your growth – as the popular saying goes, when someone "throws you under the bus."

While you may find self-sacrificial behavior in your closest personal relationships (and I hope that you do), in the corporate world, the unspoken rule is every man for himself. What looks like backstabbing, if we look through a personal lens, is a harsh reality of organizational life. Even colleagues who genuinely like you will look out for themselves if your best interests conflict with their best interests. *"Et tu, Brute?"*

Below the surface, even in the healthiest culture, lurks the possibility that you will one day feel the sharp blade of betrayal. Accepting this reality is the initial step to growing as a leader.

The first element of protection is to avoid paranoia. In most ordinary work situations, most people will behave in collaborative ways that advance everyone's best interests. If you constantly expect to be betrayed, these expectations will affect your behavior and erode interpersonal trust. A "stab or be stabbed" attitude will escalate tensions and conflict and likely result in a "stab or be stabbed" atmosphere; expectations will shape the reality.

Rather than being permanently on the defensive, you can begin to recognize the signs that backstabbing is likely to occur. Is a situation developing where the allocation of resources – time, budget, promotions, or jobs – is likely to be inadequate for everyone to get everything that they want? Does your manager have some control over or input into this situation? In battles over a shrinking pie, backstabbing is likely. Another danger sign is a failure of some sort where responsibility is not immediately clear. Not all managers will own up to their mistakes (as I suggest in Lesson 12). Instead, some will look for scapegoats. When the company gets new stakeholders or any other time office politics are likely to be important for maintaining or advancing one's position are also potential signs of danger.

The essential element of protection against backstabbing is to broaden your own relationships within the organization. Having a network of peers and potential champions allows you to be better informed about potential shifts in the office climate. Another advantage of building social capital within the organization is that it enables you to have fallback plans in place if your boss abandons the role of being your primary supporter or turns into your chief persecutor. Again, you should not expect that these new people will place your interests ahead of their own, but expanding your web of relationships increases the chances that at least one other person's interests will be aligned with your own. Having an ally in the battle will be much more powerful than going it alone.

The business world or the "corporate life" can, at times, feel like a street fight; however, understanding the Trust Factor, which I explain in the next chapter, will alleviate feelings of paranoia and isolation.

The Trust Factor – yes, you can trust.

Ernest Hemingway is often misquoted as having said, "The best way to find out if you can trust somebody is to trust them." His actual observation in a letter to a friend was that "the way to make people trustworthy is to trust them."

While the fake quote suggests taking a leap of faith, the true quote offers a system for empowering people.

Businesses spend a lot of time, effort, and money recruiting the right person for the job. The person who is hired has the credentials, knowledge, and skill to perform the job. The person understands the role expectations and job requirements. In other words, they are competent, and they got the offer because the organization believes that they have the skills and ability to meet their commitments to the organization.

Unfortunately, some bosses see things very differently. Once the person is on the job, their manager may not trust that the person really can do the job. I'm not speaking about the manager helping the new hire to progress through the expected period of adjustment to the organization or to ascend the usual learning curve in a new role. I'm referring to an unspoken trial period where the boss essentially requires the person to prove that he or she can do their job. In these cases, a manager will either boss the person around to make sure she does what she is supposed to do or scrutinize every mistake, holding it up as evidence of the person's incompetence. In either scenario, the employee is disempowered; either he or she is constrained to do only what they are told, or they are held back by fear of doing something wrong. Where is the trust?

This lack of trust is often exacerbated because of the personal qualities of the new employee, such as his or her age, race, or gender, activate biases about trust and trustworthiness. Unfortunately, Australian novelist Gregory David Roberts was right when he wrote, "A man trusts another man when he sees enough of himself in him." Many managers do not look beyond the superficial qualities in making this determination. Instead, when a person is visibly different, a manager may question whether the person really has the credentials, or he or she may have implicit (or explicit) biases that lead them to think that certain people are simply less competent. As a leader, you must root out any biases or stereotypes that might cause you to trust people from certain groups less than you would trust others. Remember Lesson 1 and the potential need for a little wart removal.

As a new employee, I encountered a lack of trust, but rather than feeling disempowered, I took agency for establishing trust in the relationship. In most cases, the leaders' inability to trust came from their own inadequacies, whether unacknowledged biases, unresolved past betrayals, or an ineffective leadership style. A leader whose style is to micromanage or to retain all the power or to rely on an image of wisdom as their sole source of influence will have difficulty trusting others. Attitudes such as "only one right way" thinking, power lust, or the need to be seen as the smartest guy in the room all drive managers to avoid any risk related to the actions of another person. Essentially, these guys cannot allow themselves to be vulnerable enough to rely on someone else.

When the other person was not inherently trusting, the way to introduce trust into the relationship was for me to be the first to trust. I showed my flawed leaders that despite their shortcomings, I had chosen to trust them. I did this by being open and transparent about myself and my values. By exposing my true self, I modeled being vulnerable. Allowing reluctant leaders to see that *I* trusted *them* often melted their distrust and shortened the trial period.

As a leader, it is even more important to me to continue to model trust for two main reasons. First, I want to foster trust within my teams. On effective teams, the members trust the leaders and each other. It would be both hypocritical and fruitless to ask my people to trust others, including me, if I constantly showed that I do not trust them.

The second reason for modeling trust brings us back to Hemingway and to another legendary figure, Steve Jobs. Jobs once said, "It doesn't make sense to hire smart people and tell them what to do; we hire smart people so they can tell us what to do."

If organizations are hiring the right people, and if leaders want to create trustworthy employees, then leaders must trust employees to the jobs they've been hired to do. Allowing employees to make the decisions and solve the problems that we hired them for provides intellectual stimulation and activates their drive and desire to accomplish more. Employees who feel intellectually stimulated put in more effort for their leaders, which means leaders can trust the employees to handle more and, thus, provide even more intellectual stimulation – a virtuous circle.

Using trust to increase individual commitment is essential for organizational success in today's global war for talent. Use the trust factor to your advantage.

Fashion vs. Style – Trendy or Trendsetter?

If you've ever had the chance to people-watch in a major city, you probably saw a few dozen (or hundred, depending on how long you watched) people with the same look. Whether wearing the same color scheme or shape or length of skirt or accessorizing with the same shoes or handbag, these fashionistas chase the latest trends to look *à la mode*, ever so fashionable and of the moment. At some point, they become almost indistinguishable.

During your people-watching, you might also have noticed a few rare women and men with a style all their own that seemed to fit them perfectly, no matter how outrageous. If not, think back to the opening scenes of *Sex in the City* and Carrie Bradshaw's pink tutu. She wore it and similarly daring outfits without a hint of self-consciousness. Her authentic style defied the popular trend and set her apart from commonplace fashionistas. Rather than being a trend follower, she was a trendsetter.

As with clothing, in leadership, we have a choice between following a fashion or developing our own style. Our clothing choices are often very deliberate, and we use them to communicate how we want others to see us. Deciding on your approach to leadership should be just as deliberate because it also communicates who you are. Do you want to fit in or do you want to be your best self even if it means standing out?

Many leadership theories and many leadership consultants who apply these theories in organizations follow rather than influence popular views. The question they ask is, "What type of leadership seems to be most effective right now?" These leadership fashion gurus generalize an ideal of leadership based on a society's current views about what people want from leaders. Many individuals spend their careers chasing the latest leadership fashion, adopting a practice of leadership that fits this moment or that moment. They imitate a leadership icon without giving much thought to whether the icon's approach to leadership is well-suited to them. Again, think of the would-be fashionista who chooses a cut of pants that's all wrong for her body type just because the ladies in *Vogue* are wearing them. Awkward!

Leaders fall into the fashion trap most often because they have not taken the time to think about how they want to lead. I have seen people thrust into leadership positions because they were good at a specific task, without much consideration of whether they would be good at leading. These sudden leaders often have little time to prepare for leadership and pick an approach that is hyped or is familiar because they've seen someone else use it. Opportunities to influence a group decision or speak up about a company practice or motivate a struggling colleague or organize a work stream all present possibilities to exercise leadership. Understanding that the leadership journey begins much earlier than we think allows us to be more deliberate in deciding what kind of leader we want to be. People often miss the opportunity to think about leadership early on because they do not realize that we can exercise leadership without having the leadership title.

On my own journey, I have not always seen these opportunities in advance. Sometimes, I recognized a moment that would forever shape my leadership identity and made deliberate choices. I could feel the spotlight shining bright and knew that what I decided to do in that moment would communicate my character to those watching me. Other times, I missed the significance of a crucial moment while it was happening and only later came to see how important the moment had been to defining me.

Even when I failed to see the critical choice in a given moment, what allowed me to make choices that were consistent with my character and my values was an early decision to focus on leadership as a relationship between leaders and followers. This focus enabled me to develop the leadership style that allows both me and my followers to bring our best selves to the relationship. I have a unique style that is right for me and that is flexible enough to adapt my behaviors to the needs of the individuals whom I lead.

My current style is a combination of authentic, inclusive, and strategic styles. I lead with my heart; I encourage and value all voices; and I keep an eye on the organization's objectives and interests, balancing these with individual employee needs. This style has consistently produced successful results for me. It is the result of my unique journey, of me defining my own path for success without trying to be somebody else.

I have resisted being a leadership fashionista. Only time will tell if I am a leadership trendsetter. For today, I have a style that fits me like a custom-made garment, precisely because it is hand-tailored by me. As I continue to grow and evolve as a leader, I may need to make alterations, but having a clear vision of what kind of leader I want to be gives me a master pattern.

I encourage you to use the pieces and threads in these 20 lessons to design, make to measure, and courageously show off your own leadership style.

The leadership challenge for you today is that no matter **the good, the bad, or the ugly** always find a golden nugget…learn the lesson. Pick up the golden nugget. Polish it so it will shine. This golden nugget will help you be your best self; a leader people will follow no matter your title. *A few shiny golden nuggets I have learned is that leadership takes heart. It takes bravery, and it takes courage.* So take it!

Made in the USA
Middletown, DE
23 October 2020